I LOVE HISTORY
Alexander the Great

Text: Anastasia D. Makri

Illustration-Activities: Eva Karantinou

Translated from Greek into English
Kiriaki Papakonstantinou
English editor
Dr Nicola Wardle

UNDER THE AEGIS OF

 United Nations Educational, Scientific & Cultural Organization

CLUB FOR UNESCO OF THE DEPARTMENT OF PIRAEUS & ISLANDS
Petrou Ralli 210 & Thiseos 1 Nikea,
Tel.: 210 4967757, Fax: 210 4944564 - www.unescopireas.gr e-mail: unescop@otenet.gr

AGYRA
publications

Alexander's childhood

When Alexander was born, the news spread like wildfire throughout the palace.

Alexander was the son of King Philip II of Macedon and Queen Olympias.

Philip was an ambitious and skillful king. His aim was to expand his kingdom. He dreamed of uniting Greece under his command and conquering Asia. One of his greatest military inventions was

the Macedonian phalanx, a nearly invincible formation of the Macedonian army (see page 17).

His best friend from childhood, was Hephaestion. The two boys were taught military skills together and in their spare time they played the lyre and read poetry. When Alexander became an adolescent, his father – Philip – hired the great Greek philosopher Aristotle as his teacher.

Aristotle contributed in a very positive manner to the moulding of Alexander's personality; the young student much admired and appreciated his teacher.

One day, Alexander asked his father to let him ride a magnificent wild horse that no one had managed to tame. His father was greatly worried by his son's wish. However, Alexander was sure he could manage

to ride it because he knew the reason why the horse reacted so violently. Before riding him, he turned the horse towards the sun so that his shadow fell behind him, having observed that he was afraid of his own shadow. Then he jumped on his back without any difficulty and started galloping. King Philip, very proud of his son and excited, gave him the horse called Bucephalus.

Alexander admired and respected his father, but Philip's attitude towards his mother troubled him. When Alexander was about twenty years old, Philip decided to get married to another woman and make her queen. This enraged Alexander. However, not long after, something terrible happened ... Philip was assassinated and so Alexander was proclaimed King of Macedon.

Alexander, King of Macedon

When Alexander became king, some Greek cities revolted. The city of Thebes was the first to revolt. Alexander, however, quickly managed to suppress the revolt and the city was razed to the ground; the only house spared was that of Pindar, the poet of whom Alexander had heard from his teacher, Aristotle. After that, the Greek city-states were subdued and acknowledged Alexander's power and authority. Alexander, however, had even greater plans. He planned to invade the Persian Empire, determined to make his father's dream – which he shared – come true. In a short time he trained a large army, built a fleet and set out for the East. The ships, in addition to soldiers and builders, carried scientists and artists.

After a long journey they reached the coast of Asia Minor. Alexander jumped ashore and plunged a spear into the sand, a gesture which symbolised his conviction that he would conquer that land.

Alexander continued southwards. However, he was soon faced with a problem: the Granicus River, on the opposite bank of which the Persian army was waiting for him. How was his army to cross the river? He found the shallowest part of the river, crossed with his men and charged the Persians. The Persians, unable to defeat Alexander's brave army, took flight. Alexander, victorious, continued his

march eastwards. No city in his path remained unconquered. Most cities welcomed him as a hero, anticipating better times ahead. Indeed, Ada, Queen of Caria welcomed him herself. Alexander, delighted with her warm welcome, let her remain on the throne.

When Alexander arrived in Gordion, he saw in the centre of the city a famous chariot. It had been tied up for years with such a complicated knot that nobody had been able to undo it. Then a resident of the city told him of a legend which said that the man who managed to undo the knot would rule the whole Asia.

"I have my own way to untie the Gordian knot," said Alexander. He took out his sword and sliced the knot in half.

Alexander conquers the East

Alexander and his army had been fighting for a whole year. Their food was running low and the difficulties they faced were numerous. Then, he decided to head towards Syria. His army, who had complete trust in their leader, followed him. However, this meant that they had to face Darius III, king of Persia, who was waiting with an army of about six hundred thousand men. The Macedonians panicked. Alexander, however, managed to identify the weakest part of the Persian army. Then, with some of his cavalry with him, he made a decisive attack on that weak position. The Persian troops were surprised and took flight. Then Alexander turned his attention to Darius who fled from the battlefield. The Persian army, without his leadership, was easily defeated.

After the battle, Alexander went to Darius' tent, which was full of incomparable treasures. Apart from the treasures, however, Darius' wife, mother and children, were also there and they knelt before him to plead for mercy; and mercy he showed.

After the army had rested, Alexander continued south. His confidence inspired his men. They conquered every city they attacked.

Eventually, they reached the island city of Tyre. There, the people were determined not to let anyone enter their island. Alexander had a causeway built in the sea, on which he put his siege engines. The Macedonian army tied a siege engine between two ships and started catapulting stones to smash holes in the walls. Thus, Alexander's army rushed into the city through these openings and forced the brave inhabitants to surrender.

Once Darius heard that Alexander had conquered Tyre as well, he panicked and sent him a message: "Stop the war now, and I'll give you half my kingdom and my daughter as your wife."

However, Alexander simply smiled and gave his answer to Darius' messenger: "Tell your king that I already have half his kingdom and, as for his daughter, I can marry her any time I want" – and the war continued...

Alexander next planned to conquer Egypt. The Egyptians welcomed him as a liberator and crowned him king. Alexander felt a strong urge to visit the temple of the Egyptian god Amon-Ra located in the Siwa Oasis in the desert. Alexander believed that Zeus and Amon-Ra were one and the same, and he wanted to talk to the priest of the temple.

When he returned he did not tell anyone what he had asked the priest. He gave his friend Hephaestion the impression that what the priest had told him was very important to him. His generals, however, speculated that the priest had asserted that Alexander had the power of a god and would conquer the world.

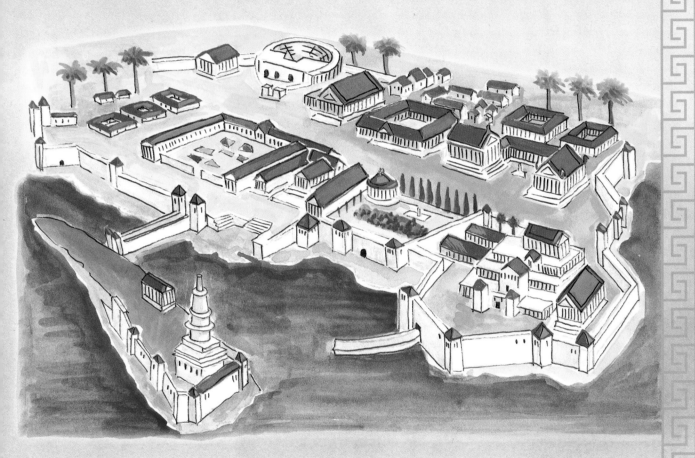

During his stay in Egypt, Alexander chose a beautiful location by the sea and founded a new city which he called Alexandria. As his conquests continued, other cities bearing his name were also built. These cities became centres of Greek culture. However, Alexander's desire was to go to Persia.

When kings clash

The Macedonians marched for months searching for Darius, until they found him at Gaugamela. This time, Darius had chosen as the battlefield a place which he had completely levelled. He had in mind Alexander's battle formation and thought that the Macedonians would use their usual weapons. He also had two hundred chariots with blades attached to their wheels. In addition, he had nails scattered on the side where the Macedonians would line up, so their horses would stumble on them as they began their attack.

The battle started and it was very fierce. Darius drove his chariots into battle. In surprise he saw the Macedonians, instead of fighting back, break ranks and disperse. The Persians' horses overtook them and were felled by the nails they had themselves put there. Then, Alexander chased Darius' chariot and killed his charioteer. Darius, however, had disappeared. Immediately afterwards, Alexander conquered the cities of Babylon and Susa and proceeded eastwards. The only way forward was a narrow path, known as the Persian Gates. It was there, the Persian army was waiting. He ordered his men to find someone who knew the area. Soon, a young, frightened shepherd was brought to him, who told him there was another passage at the top of the mountain, but that it was rather steep. When night fell, Alexander led a small group of men through that passage in the snow and got behind the Persians.

At dawn, Alexander attacked the Persians from behind, while the rest of his army attacked from the front. The Persians were taken by surprise and suffered a crushing defeat. Alexander marched on towards Persepolis, the capital of Persia, which he entered in triumph. Faced with the incredible wealth of the city, he thought of his companions who had died so that he could come so far. He immediately

urged his army to seize whatever they wanted from those treasures.

Alexander had been welcomed as a hero by the countries he had conquered. Here, however, the people disapproved of him. This enraged him and he ordered his men to burn the palace to the ground. In one night, Persepolis was reduced to ashes. On seeing the ruins, Alexander regretted his decision, but it was too late. After this he continued his pursuit of Darius. However, one of Darius' distant relatives murdered the king and had himself crowned in his place. Alexander, angered by this deed, after burying Darius with honour, ordered the murderer to be arrested and executed.

Alexander becomes the ruler of Persia

Alexander was now the king of Persia as well. His great dream had come true. His attitude, however, changed. He behaved like a Persian king and required the Macedonians bow down before him, like the Persian nobles. This angered the Macedonians. One day, Alexander was giving a banquet to the officers of his army. Cleitus, one of his friends and an officer, emboldened by the wine he had drunk, shouted: "Alexander, once you were just like us, but now you behave like a Persian king. You should know you're not the son of any god. You are the son of King Philip II, who was a better man than you."

Upon hearing these words, Alexander, grabbed a spear and stabbed Cleitus in the heart. When he realised what he had done, he burst into tears. Cleitus was a brave soldier who had once saved his life.

A royal wedding

Although Alexander was now all-powerful, Oxyartes, King of the Scythians, challenged him to a fight on a mountain. Alexander offered a large reward to the first person to reach the top of the mountain. Several soldiers volunteered to climb and many of them managed to reach the top. So, Oxyartes found himself surrounded and was forced to surrender. When Alexander saw the defeated king's beautiful daughter, Roxanne, he fell in love with her and a few months later they were married. Yet, his men were not happy with this turn of events.

Alexander in India

Alexander now ruled the largest empire in the world, but it was not enough. He wanted to conquer India as well. But, how would they cross the formidable Indus River? Alexander sent half his men ahead to find boats and the other half to cut wooden boards. Then he ordered them to tie the boats together and place the boards across them. In this way they made a floating bridge and managed to cross the river.

At the next river, however, Porus, the ruler of India, was waiting for them with hundreds of elephants trained for warfare. Alexander's men were terrified. But, once again, Alexander had a plan. Every morning the Macedonian army started crossing the river and the Indians prepared for battle. Then the Macedonians would turn back so the battle did not happen. Meanwhile, Alexander's army had discovered another passage. So, one night, Alexander led half his army over that passage and the other half started crossing the river, just like every other day.

Porus did not take it seriously and so soon he found himself trapped. Alexander was the victor once more. He sent a message to Porus asking him how he would like to be treated.

"Like a king," replied Porus with dignity.

Alexander kept his word and appointed him governor of his new province of India, under his rule.

However, an unhappy event made him very sad. Shortly after the battle, his beloved horse, Bucephalus, died. In his memory, Alexander built a new city and called it Bucephala.

The way back

Alexander, however, had no intention of stopping his conquests. This made his men rather upset as they were very tired as a

14

result of all the wars; but Alexander determinedly made for China, with an exhausted army.

Their journey was anything but easy. It was the monsoon season and rain fell incessantly. His soldiers were asking to go home, but Alexander would not listen to them. When they reached the fifth river on their route, his men refused to continue. So, Alexander was forced to consent to their return, but following another route back, in order to explore the area. Their journey through the desert was rough. They ran short of food and water. So, Alexander divided his army into three parts. One part crossed the sea; the other part crossed the mountains; and the third one, along with Alexander, crossed the desert.

A great number of his men died because of the harsh conditions. When they arrived at Susa, a Persian city, Alexander got married once more, this time to the daughter of Darius. In fact, he forced several of his officers to get married as well to daughters of noble Persians, to show their friendly intentions. To convince them, he promised them lavish gifts and held grand feasts that lasted several days.

However, on his return to Persia, Alexander found an empire beginning to revolt. It took quite some time before he regained control. It was then that his beloved friend, Hephaestion, died. Alexander's pain was so great that he had his head shaved in mourning.

Trying to overcome his grief, he started considering new campaigns. One day, when sailing on the open sea with his friends, the wind blew away his headband and it landed on a ruined building. A priest who was on board said: "That is the tomb of a king. This is a bad omen."

A few days later, Alexander fell seriously ill. He was just 33 years old ...

His generals felt that he would not survive and so ordered the soldiers to parade in front of him and say goodbye. Alexander looked at them one by one, without being able to speak. Then, one of his friends leaned over and asked him "To whom do you leave your empire?"

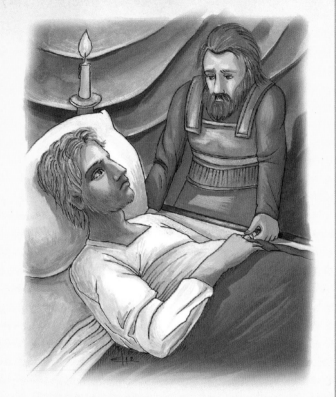

"To the best one," replied Alexander and died shortly after.

The Macedonians, overcome, put his coffin in a golden sarcophagus and started their long journey home.

A few months after Alexander's death, his widow Roxanne gave birth to a son. Eventually, they were both murdered by those who wanted to take power into their own hands. Alexander's generals fought hard over his empire trying to share it between them.

It was not long after his death that Alexander's vast empire collapsed.

A timeline of major events in the life of Alexander the Great

356 BC Alexander was born at Pella, Macedonia, to King Philip II and Olympias.

338 BC Philip conquers Greece.

336 BC Alexander is proclaimed king, after Philip's assassination.

335 BC The city of Thebes revolts.

334 BC Alexander sets out to conquer the world. His fleet sets sail for Asia and he wins his first battle at the Granicus River against Darius III of Persia.

333 BC Alexander defeats the Persians, but Darius escapes.

332 BC Alexander is welcomed as a hero in Egypt. During his visit to the coast, he founds the magnificent city of Alexandria.

331 BC Another major defeat of the Persians takes place at Gaugamela, although Darius escapes once more. Alexander enters Persepolis triumphant.

330 BC Darius is dead.

330-328 BC Alexander continues his conquest of Asia.

329 BC Alexander kills Cleitus, a faithful officer, in a fit of rage because of his criticism.

327-326 BC Alexander invades India, after defeating King Porus.

326 BC Bucephalus, his remarkable horse, dies; Alexander founds the city Bucephala in the memory of his horse.

325 BC Alexander's plans to conquer China fail, because his army refuses to go any further. He is forced to go back.

324 BC Hephaestion, his closest friend, dies. Alexander is devastated.

323 BC Alexander dies suddenly, in Babylon.

The famous "Macedonian Phalanx"

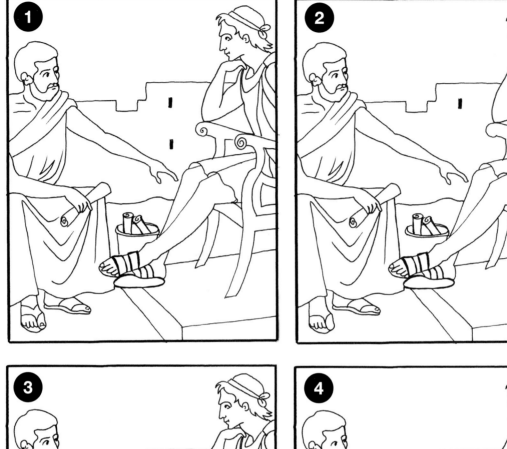

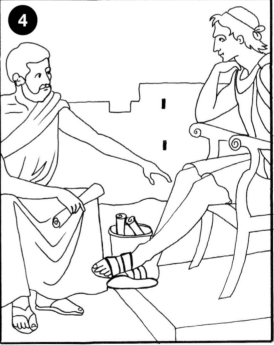

Alexander listened carefully to his teacher, the wise Aristotle.
Compare pictures 2, 3 and 4 with picture 1.
There are 5 differences in each picture. Can you spot them?

Colour the picture.

1. Alexander's horse
2. Alexander's beloved friend
3. Great Persian city where Alexander married the daughter of Darius
4. The first battle against the Persians was at the ... River.
5. The Persians were defeated in the battle that took place in ...

6. Alexander's first wife
7. He wanted to conquer this country, but he wasn't able to
8. Leader of the Persians and Alexander's serious opponent
9. Alexander's mother
10. Alexander's greatest enemies

This statue of Alexander the Great stands on the seafront in Thessaloniki. Colour the picture.

C	L	A	B	I	O	R	O	W	E	N
B	U	C	E	P	H	A	L	U	S	I
R	A	M	S	O	B	R	Y	E	Q	E
I	R	E	A	R	L	Y	M	R	U	R
D	I	V	E	U	R	O	P	M	I	A
A	S	A	S	S	E	D	I	U	F	B
Z	T	R	W	H	X	A	A	D	O	R
O	O	R	B	L	A	R	S	E	U	O
N	T	P	H	I	L	I	P	C	C	X
Q	L	O	W	E	R	U	S	K	L	A
H	E	P	H	A	E	S	T	I	O	N
O	R	L	A	V	Y	T	I	S	C	E

In the wordsearch above there are 8 names of people related to Alexander the Great. Can you find them all?

P	E	R	S	E	P	O	L	I	S	E	Y	H	Y
L	A	B	Q	U	E	W	R	N	O	L	L	E	A
Y	R	B	L	I	O	R	K	D	M	I	D	L	S
T	M	A	C	E	D	O	N	I	A	O	G	D	I
H	J	B	H	A	L	E	X	A	N	D	R	I	A
E	O	Y	I	K	O	B	S	L	D	I	E	C	O
B	B	L	N	N	G	A	U	G	A	M	E	L	A
E	R	O	A	E	I	N	S	S	L	A	C	A	N
S	A	N	D	E	N	U	A	S	O	J	E	P	S

In the wordsearch above there are the names of 11 cities or regions associated with Alexander the Great. Can you find them all?

This is the silver coin kept in the British Museum, in London.
The head of Alexander the Great is depicted on it.
Can you spot 5 differences between the two pictures?

This is the chariot to which the Gordian Knot
was tied. Colour the picture.

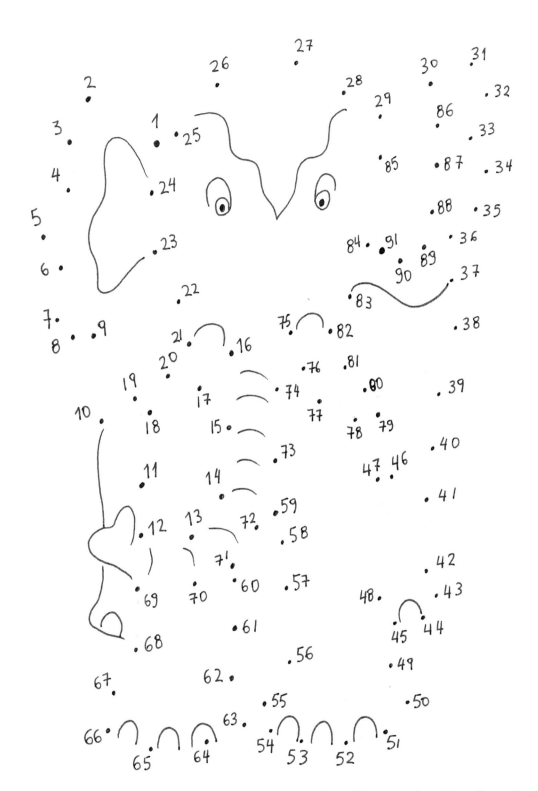

Join the dots from 1 to 91 to see what Alexander the Great saw on arriving in India.

The Seven Wonders of the Ancient World

The lighthouse of Alexandria in the famous city built by Alexander the Great on the coast of Egypt, is one of the seven wonders of the ancient world. Can you identify the other six wonders? Fill in their names.

1. THE LIGHTHOUSE OF ALEXANDRIA

2. THE _____

_____

_____

3. THE _____

_____

_____

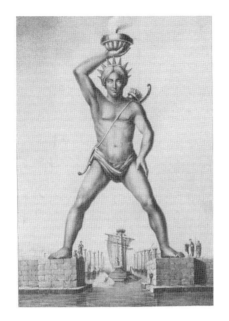

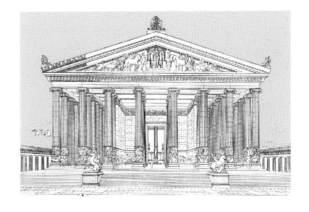

4. THE

5. THE

6. THE

7. THE

Join the dots from 1 to 95 to see what Bucephalus is afraid of.
Then, you can colour the picture.

28

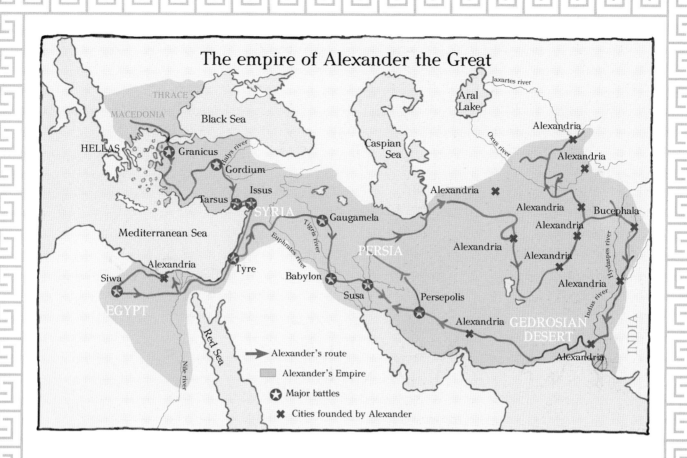

The empire of Alexander the Great

1. _ _ _ _ _ _ _ _
A N D I A M O C E

2. _ _ _ _ _ _ _
N Y B L O B A

3. _ _ _ _
A S S U

4. _ _ _ _ _
S U S S I

5. _ _ _ _ _ _ _ _ _
R I D A L A X E N A

6. _ _ _ _ _ _ _ _ _
R O L E S P I S E P

7. _ _ _ _ _ _ _ _
A C H U B A P L E

8. _ _ _ _
T R Y E

9. _ _ _ _ _ _ _
G L A M U G E A

10. _ _ _ _ _ _ _
G R U M I D O

Unscramble the letters, to find the cities and regions
through which Alexander passed. Use the map to help you.

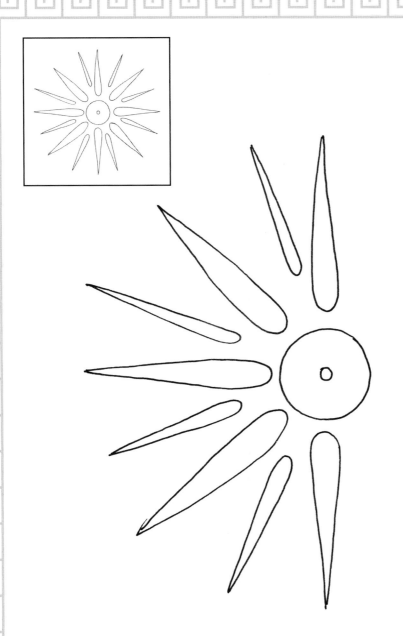

The great archaeologist Manolis Andronikos, during his excavations at Vergina, in Macedonia, discovered in 1977 the tomb of King Philip II. In this important excavation a golden chest, called a larnax, was also found. A star called «The Sun of Vergina» was hammered onto its top and is considered to be the symbol of the Greek kingdom of Macedon. The golden larnax and all the spectacular finds of the excavation are exhibited in the Archaeological museum of Vergina.
Complete the design and then colour it.

This is Darius, the Persian king.
Colour the picture.

SOLUTIONS

PAGE 18

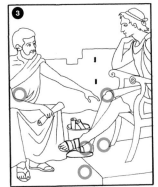

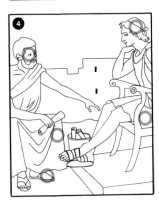

PAGE 20

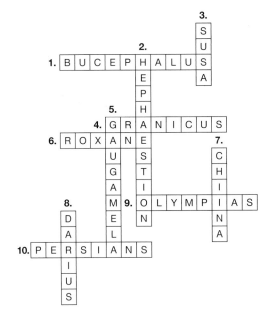

PAGE 22

PAGE 23

PAGE 27 The other 6 wonders of the ancient world were the following:

2. THE HANGING GARDENS OF BABYLON
3. THE GREAT PYRAMID OF GIZA
4. THE COLOSSUS OF RHODES
5. THE TEMPLE OF ARTEMIS AT EPHESUS
6. THE MAUSOLEUM AT HALICARNASSUS
7. THE STATUE OF ZEUS AT OLYMPIA

PAGE 29 The words are:

1. MACEDONIA
2. BABYLON
3. SUSA
4. ISSUS
5. ALEXANDRIA
6. PERSEPOLIS
7. BUCEPHALA
8. TYRE
9. GAUGAMELA
10. GORDIUM

Cover and interior design: Efthimis Dimoulas
© 2012 D.A. PAPADIMITRIOU S.A. «AGYRA» Publications
This edition, March 2019
271 L. Katsoni str. • Ag. Anargiroi P.O. 135 62 Athens, Greece • Tel.: +30 210 2693800-4 - Fax: +30 210 2693806-7
e-mail: info@e-agyra.gr • www.e-agyra.gr
ISBN 978-960-547-011-1 • Produced in Greece